Adrift

Poems & Musings

By
Diane Marie-Louise

I0171471

**Bird Brain
Publishing**

To Delight, Instruct, and Inspire

Praise for *Adrift: Poems & Musings*

"Diane Marie-Louise dares to dive deeply into the daunting depths of depression with both feet while holding her arms stretched toward the hope that shines like a lighthouse for those trying to find their way. May her poems be a beacon for the lost ones stuck in their dark night."
– Tim Heerdink, author of *Red Flag and Other Poems*

"Diane draws the reader into a vivid world full of imagery and emotion. The flow and rhythm of her poems are non-traditional, yet beautiful and easy to follow. Any reader will be able to share in the sentiments she portrays in this fantastic collection of poetry." – Charley Todd, author, editor, educator, and Municipal Liason for NaNoWrimo

"This collection of poems exemplifies a deeply brutal and honest look at issues in life that plague us all. Diane's poems make the reader journey through every human emotion moving from the darkness into the light."
– Tammy Vick, author of *Retribution*

"Whether painfully searching for answers, or giving voice to a deep longing for connection, meaning and understanding; Diane's poetry gently draws you in and bids you follow along on an inner and outer journey of what it means to be human. Honest, vulnerable, authentic, and true… you will find yourself nodding your head in identification as you meditate on these beautiful poems."
– M. Grace Bernardin, Author of *Odd Numbers*

"The author's poetry placed me in a deep and reflective state. *Learning to Let Go* brilliantly captures the emotions of aging while *It's Synonymous* reveals a witty style. I loved the rhythm of *Heart Music*. These poems are well worth a read!" – John Schneider

"Diane Marie-Louise presents the reader and hearer with words that trouble the soul and stir the heart. Her works are blunt reminders that out of suffering, alienation, and even personal horror, there is a beacon of hope – though it may be on a craggy rock in the midst of thick fog upon an endless sea." – The Publisher

ADRIFT: Poems and Musings is a collection of poems which chronicles the author's rapid descent into clinical depression, and her slow but steady and triumphant climb through acceptance and peace into serenity and contentment. A lighthouse, on the shores of Charlevoix's Lake Michigan beach, is her beacon in the night.

Adrift

Poems & Musings

By
Diane Marie-Louise

Bird Brain Publishing

To Delight, Instruct, and Inspire

Bird Brain Publishing, Evansville, Indiana
www.birdbrainpublishing.com

*The Poem *Faith* by Patrick Overton, used with permission from the author, Patrick Overton, from *The Leaning Tree,* copyright 1975 PatrickOverton.com; pmoverton@msn.com

Cover Art / Graphic Design by Regent Promotions, Evansville, Indiana

Printed in the United States of America
First Printing August 2018

Library of Congress Cataloging-in-Publication Data

Marie-Louise, Diane
    Adrift: Poems & Musings / Diane Marie-Louise
Summary:

Adrift: Poems & Musings is a collection of poems which chronicles the author's rapid descent into clinical depression, and her slow but steady and triumphant climb through acceptance and peace into serenity and contentment. A lighthouse, on the shores of Charlevoix's Lake Michigan beach, is her beacon in the night.

ISBN-13: 978-1-937668-70-9
ISBN-10: 1-937668-70-3

Faith

hen we walk to the edge of all the light we have
d take that first step into the darkness of the unknown,
e must believe one of two things will happen:

There will be something solid for us to stand upon,
or, we will be taught how to fly.

Patrick Overton
The Leaning Tree, 1976

For All those Adrift in the World

CONTENTS

Adrift

Floating without being either moored or steered. Without purpose or guidance.

Lost and confused

Darkness swirls around me
A weight that can't be lifted
Dragging me down into its depths

Yet I am still whirling around on an aimless journey
Buffeted and bruised by things I cannot see
I should fight to stay afloat,
But why?

Helpless or hopeless,
It's all the same
And it never ends

Unless I end it
Until I do

Goodbye

When all I am is said and done

And nothing left to lose

I'll walk no more in shadowed light

Nor on the path I'd choose

But stumble through my darkness

To a place where I don't care

No pain is mine forever more

And death will find me there

Misfit Toys

I am Trapped

Behind lids that won't open when strange voices and foreign sounds pound me into an awareness of being

By firm hands and soft voices murmuring, "Big stick, sweetie," as a hypodermic needle plunges through already bruised skin and errant nerve endings in search of an artery

By a bad decision and a flash of bravado that resulted in a stream of baby-sitters, prying cameras, shower doors that won't lock, mistrust, suspicion, and confusing guilt

Psyche Ward
Mental Health Unit
Lock Down
Rest

All point to people you walk quickly past, averting your eyes
Yelling people
Cursing people
People who share way too much and seek way too much attention
You want to go home
To get away before they suck out your soul until you become just like them

You don't see that you are them
Trapped in a nightmare you caused but can't end
Trapped with the throwaways and misfits who call this Hell a home

Trapped On the Island of Misfit Toys

Lost

How do I know where I'm going

When I never really knew where I've been

With head down, and blinders on

Moving from A to B to C as expected

Keeping eyes lowered

Watching one foot in front of the other

The path may have changed; I didn't care

The feet were the same

A part of me I've known all my life

Feet don't fail me now

So I followed where they led

Without knowing or caring why

But feet don't see

They walk

Into things, if the eye doesn't see

And my eyes don't look

Not because I don't care, but

Because I am afraid

Close your eyes and jump

Keep them closed and walk

To where?

I don't know

I am lost

<u>Still Untitled</u>

I'm standing at the crossroads of an undiscovered life.
I think that's a song lyric. Or if it's not, it should be.
It's not; I checked.
Maybe it will be. Maybe I could write it. Maybe I could
sing it.
Maybe I could sprout wings and a propeller and fly to
the moon.
All are equally likely.

Pretentious much? Or just cynical?
Maybe tired. Definitely overwhelmed.
All or more than one of the above?
I don't know. I can never choose.
Thus the dilemma that is my life.

The crossroads theme resonates in everything I do.
I can't make decisions.
Firstly, I hate conflict.
So any decision I make has to make everyone, even
people I don't know, happy.
Secondly, I'm a perfectionist.
So every decision I make has to be the right choice, but I
don't know what that is.
So I waffle. Vacillate. Weigh my options. Equivocate.
Because I don't know. About anything.
I'm standing at the crossroads of an undiscovered life.
Pro- or Anti-? For or Against? With or Without?
I see all sides, and can't take a stand.
I am weak. Or an empath, to put a semi-positive spin on it.
That's not necessarily a good thing.

A wise man once told me, "To decide not to decide is a
decision."

That is a quote. Paraphrased. By Harvey Cox. I looked it up.
I don't know Harvey, or whether the quote I quoted originated with him.
Should I cite it?
Maybe.
I don't know.
I can't decide.

I'm standing at the crossroads of an undiscovered life.
Which path do I take?
I sit, my back against the wooden signpost, which is surprisingly cool in the midday sun.
I meditate. I ruminate. I procrastinate.

To the right?
To the left?
Straight ahead is straight-forward, and I don't do that.
There. One decision made.
But what if I'm wrong?

Back along the road I came from, tail between my legs, never moving forward?
It's safe. It's easy. It's soul-sucking.
Never to learn, to grow, to live
Should I stay or should I go?
That's definitely a song lyric, but also a question.
One for which I have no answer.

I'm standing at the crossroads of an undiscovered life.
I stand, unmoving. Wondering. Waiting.

For what?
For now.

Forever.

What I Heard

Just leave, go away. No one wants you here.
No, you didn't say it.
You didn't say anything to me; you never do.
But I heard it.
The words you don't say echo the loudest.

Good job! You handled that well.
Yeah, that's what you said.
But what you meant was, "That's not what I would have done.
What were you thinking?"
That's what I hear in my head

I'll see you later
That's what you say
We're going out, and we don't want you to come with
That's what I hear
Over and over as I walk to my car, alone

I'm really busy today
It's not a good time, but later?
I hear the words
I see the texts
Go away. Leave me alone.
What I heard may not be what you said
But it's what you meant.

I know what I heard
The words you don't say echo the loudest

<u>RBF</u>

When you're told, by those who took the time to get to know you that they used to think you were stuck up; a snob. But you never were.

When you want to join in, but have such low self-esteem that you wait for the invitation that almost never comes. Ever.

When you see friends gathering, passing you by to sit/talk with their preferred friends while you die a little inside because you know you'll be alone, again, and you should certainly be used to it by now, but you're not. Why?

Because your smile seems forced, and sometime it is, but your natural expression of interest and contemplation is perceived as Resting Bitch Face.

Ode to a Bobo Doll

The clown-faced balloon, weighted with sand
Wobbles, grinning, daring you to punch him
You do
He gets knocked down; he gets back up again
Lather. Rinse. Repeat.
Why?
He's going to go down again.
Children shout with glee as they pummel him.
Again and again.

And again he rises, taking more abuse.
He won't stay down, even though he knows the fists are
coming.
Until they don't, because the children are bored
They walk away
The Bobo Doll waits
He wants to be knocked down
It's his job
It's why he exists
He knows no other way
He thinks he is fun
Resilient
He doesn't know he is doomed

Someone, at some time, will let the air out of the Bobo
doll
And he will rise no more
He has nothing left to give
Deflated
Defeated

<u>Uncertainty</u>

How do I know where I belong when I don't really know who I am?

Will they like me when I get there if I don't really like me now?

I need to become my own best friend before reaching out to anyone for, if they reach back, I know I'll just let go.

Not because I want to, but because

I'm scared.

I need a sign from someone, anyone, to let me know it's going to be okay.

That I'm going to be okay.

Anyone?

Crickets

Ghost Story

I had a friend
I really did
For a very long time
Although, looking back, she was my friend
But I'm not sure I was hers
I was there for her
In good times and in bad
In recent years, there were far more of the latter
I was her rock
Her loyalties, and her memory, were more fluid
Often to the point of gas-lighting

One day, I didn't have that friend
For about two months
Until she needed me
We were friends again
Always on her terms, but I didn't deserve more
She taught me that, and I believed
Until we disagreed
I think, in retrospect, that she was testing me
I failed

She ghosted me
Unfriended me on Facebook, then blocked me
Texts and calls from me went unanswered
When I saw her, she looked through me
Unspeaking
As though I were a ghost

Ghosting
I hadn't heard that term at the time it happened to me

Ending a personal relationship with someone by
suddenly and without explanation withdrawing from all
communication
That's what Google tells me
It's there in black and white
But my heart needs more
Closure

Because I think it's happening again.
Not a life-long relationship like the first one
But deeper, perhaps
A friend who got me
Was not judgmental
Was there for me as often as I was there for her
Until she wasn't
Not a clean break, but a definite withdrawal of
communication
Hers, not mine
I text; she answers selectively
She shows up when it's convenient
Which may or may not be when she says she will

Ghosted again?
I truly don't know
I feel translucent, rather than transparent
But the pain is still the same
The unbearable uncertainty
Ghost or not, I feel pain
It sucks

Two Minutes

It's noon, and the streetlights have just blinked on

Confused cicadas commence their canticle

Every doorway is filled with curious people

Raising cautiously shaded eyes to the sky

Cars, trucks, and service vehicles line the shoulder of the highway

No one speaks

No need to listen

Just watch the miracle in the sky

Two minutes seem like an eternity

Yet not nearly long enough

The moment is gone

Those gathered disperse

The moment is gone, and the day begins anew

Gone but not forgotten

Eclipse

Beacon

A fire or light set up in a high or prominent position as a warning,
signal, or celebration.

A light in the dark

A faint glow, perceived rather than seen, through heavy-
lidded eyes
I blink
Am I dreaming?
The light is stronger
Warmer
Should I be afraid?

Deafening stillness replaces the
Cacophony of confusion that has been
My spirit's song for so long

I want to reach out
But I'm more afraid of shattering what I'm sure is
An illusion of peace
I wait
Holding my breath

My heart beat drums in my ears
I can feel the blood pulsing
Warming my fingers and toes
I'd forgotten the sensation
Of living
Of being alive
Of wanting to be alive

The light so bright it warms my body
And my soul
Serenity
Peace
A tranquil calm I almost recognize
A light shines in the darkness
Helping to find my way back
Leading me home

It's Synonymous

Is it cheating if I use a Thesaurus?

I know what I mean

But I can't find the words

I'm close, and it should be good enough

It's not

It needs to be perfect

Flawless

Impeccable

No, none of those are right

Correct

Accurate

Exact. Yes.

Learning to Let Go

My mother still knows who I am
And misses my father terribly
Some days she wants to stay in bed
Other days she wants to die

She used to be critical
Nothing was good enough to meet
Her impossibly high standards
Now she is grateful
For every visit, every phone call
Every smile that comes her way
"Whatever you say."
Ever eager to please
"Just tell me what you want me to do."

"Where did you go to high school?"
She asks
Countless times
Again and again
She doesn't remember that she can't remember
Her caregivers answer her patiently
With that smile she treasures so

I'm learning to do the same.
To smile and nod
Coaxing and encouraging
Redirecting rather than
Correcting her memories and her words
Conversations
Of any kind
Make her happy.
They make me sad

My mother is slipping away
I miss her already.
But she is happy in the past
And she visits there
More and more often
Staying for longer periods of time
Still fiercely competitive
A fire in her eyes until
Confusion blinks again
I see the animation leave her smile
But I know she is content

I'm learning to be the same

Words With Friends

Words come easily to me
They form in my brain and shoot out my mouth
Sometime with a filter, but often without

Week after week, I sit here in the café
Surrounded by people I do not know
Alone with my thoughts
The words I conjure make their way to my hands and are
Deposited into the memory of my laptop

I'm used to flying solo
I don't like it, but it's how I roll

Rolled

Tonight, I'm surrounded by writing friends
One of whom I know
Two I do not
And my mind is a blank
No words except these
I have the companionship I craved

But my inspiration has gone missing
Temporarily
It's an even trade

Victory

Quitters never win
Winners never quit
That's what they say
You know, the ubiquitous They who say stuff
Everyone listens to Them
Citing them frequently
Usually inaccurately

Saying something often enough doesn't make it true

Sometimes, the only way to win is to quit
Sometimes, losing is winning

It depends on the prize
It depends on the price

If at first you don't succeed, etc.
It is better to have loved and lost, and so on
Really?
Is it healthy to fight a losing battle?
To lose, in the battle, your sense of self?
Your sanity?
If the answer is "No," then quit

This is not your battle
Not your war

Those who run away may live to fight another day
This is victory

Heart Music

Can you hear me whistling
On the outside of the wind?
Happy thoughts, too sweet to share
But I don't care
Who's listening?
Can you hear me singing
On a moonbeam from the sky?
A melody, too rich for words
But I don't care
Who's listening?
Can you hear my pulse jump
When a smile leaps to my face?
I'm full of song, and nothing's wrong
And I don't care
For I must share
The music in my heart

Charlevoix

In times of deepest darkness

I visit my Happy Place

Warm sun and cool breeze

Sunbeams chasing away goosebumps

Sounds of seagulls and harbor bells

Water lapping against the wooden docks

White sails against the blue sky

Flying across clear water

Grains of pure white sand caress my feet

The smell of freshwater fish permeates the air

And brings me home

Lake of Serenity

Water

Cool, crisp, clear

Bracingly cold

Even in the summer sun

Three feet in and I can still count my toes

On sand rippled by gentle waves

Lapping against the shore

Like a mother's heartbeat

Waves

Calm, Gentle, Serene

The sound carries me back to

Childhood summers

I was happy then

I emerge, shivering, to stand on the

Beach

The warm, white, and silken sand

The sound of distant boats and

The piercing cry of the gulls

Peace is mine, and

I am happy again

<u>Be Kind. Always.</u>

We must be kind to one another

To learn when to

Agree to disagree with

Respect

Seeking to help those who need

But will not seek

To give of ourselves generously

Not looking for praise or recompense

But because we are able

And we are

Kind

We Are Family

Family is formed
Not by blood
Not by heritage
Not by location or predisposition
But by Faith
That we belong together

We believe
We love
We value
We support

Because together
As a family
We are invincible

Diane Marie-Louise is an author and poet. Her other works can be found in *The River City Writers Present Crossroads: An Anthology of Stories*, and her soon-to-be released novel *Lost and Found?*

Readers may contact the author at:
dianemarielouise.writer@gmail.com

Bird Brain Publishing

To Delight, Instruct, and Inspire

www.ingramcontent.com/pod-product-compliance
Lightning Source LLC
Chambersburg PA
CBHW020607030426
42337CB00013B/1251